Cool Scrapbooks

Pam Price

ABDO
Publishing Company

visit us at
www.abdopub.com

Published by ABDO Publishing Company, 4940 Viking Drive, Edina, Minnesota 55435. Copyright © 2005 by Abdo Consulting Group, Inc. International copyrights reserved in all countries. No part of this book may be reproduced in any form without written permission from the publisher. Checkerboard Library is a trademark and logo of ABDO Publishing Company.

Printed in the United States.

Design and Production: Mighty Media, Inc.
    Cover Photo: Anders Hanson
    Interior Photos: Anders Hanson, Brand X, Comstock, Corbis, Photo Disc
    Series Coordinator: Pam Scheunemann
    Art Direction: Tracy Kompelien

Library of Congress Cataloging-in-Publication Data

Price, Pamela S.
    Cool scrapbooks / Pam Price.
      p. cm. -- (Cool crafts)
    ISBN 1-59197-744-4
    1. Photographs--Conservation and restoration--Juvenile literature. 2. Photograph albums--Juvenile literature. 3. Scrapbooks--Juvenile literature. I. Title. II. Series.

TR465.P75 2004
745.593--dc22

2004046290

Scrapbook tools, materials, and design assistance provided by Scrapbooks Too, Bloomington, MN. Special thanks to Susan and Minda!

For Your Safety

Some of the tools shown in this book should be used only when an adult is present.

Contents

Boldfaced words throughout the text are defined in the glossary.

Introduction

A scrapbook uses photographs to tell a story. But a scrapbook is more than a collection of photographs. In a scrapbook, we add words and decorative elements to the photographs. This helps us tell the story and express our feelings about that story.

Scrapbooks are very personal. That's because you decide which memories you want to preserve. You tell your own story and decide how to tell it. You decide which pictures and words to include. You decide how simple or complex you want each page to be.

This book shows you the materials and techniques you need to get started. It discusses which materials will help preserve your photographs. It covers techniques for working with photos. You'll learn how to assemble pictures and words to create a basic page. And you'll learn how to decorate your pages with a wide assortment of **embellishments**.

What this book won't tell you is what should go on each page. That's because the scrapbook you're creating is your own. Your imagination and creativity will help you to create a scrapbook that's as unique as you are!

The History of Scrapbooks

Scrapbooks have been around for centuries. Before photographs were common, people filled scrapbooks with quotations, poems, dried flowers, and newspaper clippings. Early scrapbooks were called common-place books.

Friendship books were popular in Victorian times. Young women placed intricate weavings made from their friends' hair in their books. They also included autographs and diary entries about their friends.

Some very famous people kept scrapbooks. Thomas Jefferson filled many scrapbooks with articles about his presidency. Mark Twain invented and patented a scrapbook with self-pasting pages.

The name scrapbook probably comes from the brightly colored paper that people called **scrap**. These were mostly printed labels and cards. Many people also collected **die cuts** in their scrapbooks. Die cuts are sheets of pre-cut colorful paper shapes. Today, people still enjoy decorating their scrapbooks with die cuts.

However, memories are the true link between the scrapbooks of then and now. We keep scrapbooks to preserve memories for ourselves and for future generations.

Scrapbooks & Paper

Scrapbooks and paper pages come in many sizes and styles. Here are some things to consider when choosing.

Scrapbooks

Most scrapbooks have pages that are 12 inches (30 cm) square or 8½ by 11 inches (22 by 28 cm). Smaller scrapbooks are nice for making theme scrapbooks, such as vacation scrapbooks.

Sleeves

Most scrapbooks have clear plastic sleeves that you slip your pages into. Be sure to choose sleeves that are archival quality. Scrapbooks with paper pages are still available, but are less popular.

Bindings

You should decide what type of binding you want on your scrapbook. Your choices include ring binders and books with straps or posts to hold the pages. These can be opened up so you can add or rearrange pages. You cannot do this with spiral-bound books.

Paper

You will use a wide variety of paper to create pages and accents for your scrapbook. Always choose paper that is archival quality.

Cardstock

Cardstock comes in many colors and patterns. This sturdy paper is used as a base for pages and for making **mats**. Most scrapbooking stores have cardstock in 12-inch squares and 8½- by 11-inch sheets.

Decorative paper

Decorative paper is not as heavy as cardstock. However, you can still use it as a base for pages. You can also cut it into smaller pieces to make **embellishments**. Decorative paper comes in even more colors and patterns than cardstock.

Vellum

Vellum is a transparent paper. Many scrapbookers like to write on vellum and lay it over the photos. Because it is transparent, you can still see the pictures beneath it.

Other specialty papers include handmade paper, suede paper, and metallic paper. These are more expensive papers and used to create special themes.

What Does Archival Quality Mean?

Archival quality means that the materials won't damage your photos. Archival-quality materials are acid free. Look for the words archival quality or photo safe on all your scrapbooking materials. That includes sleeves, pages, papers, adhesives, and inks.

Basic Tools & Materials

The array of tools and materials available is overwhelming. Keep it simple when you're getting started. Buy only the materials you need right now.

Adhesives

The adhesives you use will depend on what you are trying to do. Some adhesives are permanent. Others are removable. Use removable adhesive on pictures that are one of a kind.

Photo tape

Photo tape is sticky on both sides. You have to peel the backing off one side of the tape to use it.

Tape rollers

Tape rollers dispense tape that is sticky on both sides. And, you don't have to peel off the backing. Use tape rollers to attach photos and paper.

Glue sticks

Glue sticks are drier than liquid glue and will not buckle paper. They are easy to use and dry quickly.

Glue pens

Glue pens are great for putting glue on small pieces of paper. The size of the tip controls how much glue comes out.

Cutting Tools

Scissors are the basic tool you will use to cut paper and crop photos. However, there are many specialized cutters that you may want to try.

Scissors
You need regular paper scissors for cutting and trimming paper. Use small scissors, such as nail scissors or embroidery scissors, for cutting silhouettes.

Decorative-edge scissors
Decorative-edge scissors have blades that cut patterns. There are many patterns available.

Paper trimmers
Paper trimmers make straight cuts in paper and photos. Some scrapbooking stores provide paper trimmers for their customers to use while working in the store.

Templates
A **template** is a pattern that you can trace. There are templates for cutting shapes, making letters, and drawing designs. Nested templates contain the same shape in many sizes.

Mats
Use a self-healing cutting **mat** underneath cutters to protect the paper and the work surface underneath. Use a pounding mat for punching holes and setting **eyelets**.

Pens

You will use pens to draw and to add titles, captions, and **journal** entries to your pages. Use only **pigment** pens. The pigment ink won't fade or run. The size and shape of the tip determine what kind of line it marks.

Journaling pens

Choose a black pigment pen for journaling. Test several in the store to see which you like best.

Vanishing ink

Use vanishing ink for marking cutting lines and layout lines.

Colored pencils

You may want to use colored pencils to decorate your pages. Choose pencils that are water resistant and fade resistant.

Materials to Avoid

These materials are not recommended for use in scrapbooks.

- ▸ Rubber cement
- ▸ Masking tape
- ▸ Transparent tape
- ▸ Crepe paper
- ▸ Construction paper

Special Tools & Materials

You can create a very nice scrapbook using only photos, paper, scissors, glue, and a pen. However, specials tools and materials can add fun and creativity.

Stickers

Stickers come in just about any theme, size, and shape you can imagine.

Embossing tools

Use an embossing **template** and embossing tool to create raised designs.

Punches

Use punches to make small, perfect shapes in paper. They come in many patterns.

Tip

Punch through waxed paper a couple of times to lubricate sticky blades. Punch through aluminum foil or very fine sandpaper to clean and sharpen the blades.

Stencils

Use paint or markers with stencils to create letters or shapes.

Die cuts

You can buy just one **die cut** or a set. Some craft stores have die cut machines. They will make simple die cuts from paper you select.

Eyelets

Use **eyelets** as an accent or to attach elements to a page. You need a punch and an eyelet tool to fasten them.

Taking Care of Your Tools & Materials

- ▶ Store your scrapbook in an upright position.
- ▶ Store your paper away from light and moisture. If possible, store it flat.
- ▶ Cap your pens tightly to keep them from drying out.
- ▶ Replace the caps on adhesives to keep them from drying out. Store them away from heat and sun.
- ▶ Organize your tools so you know what you have and where it is.
- ▶ Clean and dry rubber stamps, rulers, and templates each time you use them.

Design Basics

Layout refers to how you arrange things on a page. Planning a layout is done by trial and error. You gather your materials and try different arrangements until you like what you see. Here are some design principles to help you design your pages.

Pick a Theme and Stick to It

Each page in your scrapbook tells a short story. You will have to edit what you put on each page. That means you evaluate each item you could put on the page and decide whether it really belongs or not. For each page, choose only items that help tell that story. There's an old saying that might help, "If in doubt, leave it out."

Sometimes you need more than one page to tell the story. In that case, plan a layout that uses two facing pages. Two pages that face each other are called a **spread**. Design both pages at the same time. That way your theme and design will be consistent.

Sample Themes

Here are some sample themes to get you started.

- ▸ Birthday
- ▸ Holiday
- ▸ Vacation
- ▸ New brother or sister
- ▸ Things you like
- ▸ Your team
- ▸ Field trip
- ▸ Party
- ▸ Favorite food
- ▸ Friends

Keep It Simple

Putting too many elements on a page creates clutter. You don't know where to look or what's important. Leave some space open for the eyes to rest on. This is called white space.

Create a Focal Point

The focal point is the thing on a page that draws your eye to it. You want your most important photo to be the focal point. To emphasize that photo, you can make it bigger than the others. You can place it higher on the page. Or, you can give it a **mat** that is different from the others.

Vary Shapes and Sizes

Vary the shape and size of elements on a page. That makes the page more interesting to look at. We tend to look at the biggest thing or the different thing on a page first. Then we look at the other things. This is one way you can highlight your focal point.

Texture

Adding texture to a page makes it more interesting. You can do this by layering materials. You can add materials that have texture, like fabric, yarn, or handmade paper. You can also create the illusion of texture by using patterned papers. Again, keep it simple.

This page follows the basics of good design. Everything on the page relates to the birthday theme. The photo is clearly the focal point. The sticker border at the bottom anchors the page. The happy birthday sticker acts as both a title and a decorative element. The cupcake die cut adds texture.

Balance

In design, balance refers to size and proportion. To understand this, it helps to think of a seesaw. Two small kids can balance one big kid on a seesaw. Likewise, you can use several small elements to visually balance a large element on a page.

Color and texture affect balance too. A small, brightly colored photo will balance a large photo with soft colors. A small piece of handmade paper with **journaling** has a lot of visual texture. It will balance a larger photo.

Color

Color is often the hardest part of designing a page. That's because there are so many to choose from! Limit the number of colors you put on one page. You want color to highlight your focal point, not compete with it.

The simple way to pick colors is to just try different color combinations until you find one you like. Pick a main color first. It may be a color that's in your photo. Then pick one or two accent colors.

You will use a lot of your main color and less of your accent colors. If you use the same amount of each color, it can draw attention away from the photo.

This page is a mess. All the elements relate to the birthday theme. But, there is so much clutter that it's hard to know where to look. Stickers are meant to accent a page. These stickers draw attention away from the photograph. Some croppers call a page like this a "sticker sneeze."

All about Photos

Photographs are the heart of the scrapbook. Take the time to choose good pictures that help tell the story. Here are some things to consider when choosing photos for your scrapbook.

Copies

Make sure that any photo you use in your scrapbook is not the only copy. This is particularly important with historical family photos. There are several ways to get photographs copied. You can have the photo scanned and printed. You can make copies on a color copier. You can also have new prints made from the original negative.

Composition

Composition refers to how and where a subject is placed in a photograph. Is the background interesting, or does it overwhelm the subject? Is the subject the focal point of the picture? Is the subject somewhat centered? You can often crop a picture to make it look better.

Keep It Clean

Here is how to keep your photos looking good.

- Wash your hands to remove any ink, glue, or dirt.
- Handle photos by their edges to avoid getting fingerprints on them.
- Work on a clean, dry surface.

The photo on the left is poorly composed. The subject is off center and a tree limb blocks her face. The photo on the right is more pleasing to look at. The subject is centered and nicely framed by the window.

Cropping

Cropping is cutting away the parts of the photo you don't want. However, never crop original, one-of-a-kind, or historical photos. Crop a copy instead.

Color or Black-and-White?

Don't overlook black-and-white pictures. They look especially nice against colorful pages and **mats**. Some people also prefer black-and-white pictures for family history pages.

To make a black-and-white photo look antique, scan it. Then use photo-editing software to give the photo a sepia tone. Sepia is a yellowish brown color.

To Mat or Not to Mat?

Not every picture has to have a mat. Sometimes you might mat just the main picture. Other times you may decide to mat all the pictures, but to give the main picture a double mat. There is no rule here. Just do what looks good to you.

Usually one-eighth to one-quarter inch (3–7 mm) of the mat shows. Sometimes you may want more to show. A rule of thumb is that if the picture is large, more of the mat should show. And if the picture is small, there should be less mat showing.

no mat

¼-inch mat

⅛-inch mat

Cropping & Matting

Learning how to crop and mount photographs is an important part of scrapbooking. You can use these techniques for cutting and mounting other items on your pages too.

Silhouette Photos

1. Use small, sharp scissors to cut out your picture. Mount the trimmed photo on a **mat** with photo tape.

2. Use a Magic Matter™ to mark the cut lines. Place the pencil tip in the disk opening. Then gently move the disk and pencil around the photo.

In the Round

Use a compass to crop and mat round photos. Place the point of the compass in the center of the photo. Spread the compass and slowly turn it to mark the crop line. Trim the photo and mat it. Then spread the compass a quarter-inch wider to mark the cut line on the mat.

Square and Rectangular Photos

1. Use a ruler and a pencil to mark cutting lines.

2. Use a paper trimmer or sharp scissors to make the cuts.

3. Use a paper trimmer to cut a **mat** that is a slightly wider and higher than the photograph. For a double mat, cut a second mat slightly bigger than the first one.

4. Apply photo tape to the back of the photo. Position the photo over the mat. Press gently to set the adhesive.

Adding Words

It's said that a picture is worth a thousand words. But adding a few words to your pages can help you tell the story even better!

A title sets the mood for the page. **Journaling** lets you say something about why the story is important to you. Single words scattered here or there add emphasis.

You can use a stencil to trace a title right on your page.

Titles

A title should give an idea of what the story is about. It can be funny, silly, or serious. The title should be bigger than other words on the page. But it shouldn't be so big that it draws attention from the pictures.

There are many ways to add a title to a page.

- Write it by hand.
- Use a stencil to trace the letters onto the page.
- Use a stencil to make letters that you cut out and glue on.
- Print out a title on the computer and glue it to the page.

You can also stencil the title on contrasting paper, then cut it out.

Journaling

Journaling adds a personal touch to your pages. It allows you to tell a story about what's in the pictures. Sometimes it's hard to decide what to write on a page. To get started, try this exercise. Ask yourself, who, what, where, when, why, and how? For example, if you are doing a page about a family trip, consider writing about these questions.

- Who went on the trip? Who did you meet there?

- What happened on the trip? What is happening in the photos on the page? What did you like or dislike about the trip?

- Where did you go? Where were the photos on the page taken?

- When were you there?

- Why did you like this vacation? Why would you go there again?

- How did you decide to go there? How did what you see in the photos happen? How did you get there?

You don't have to write about all of these things. In fact, some journaling is quite short. One sentence may be all you need to say. But working through all the questions does help you decide what's important to you and what you want to write about.

This year we went to the Bahamas for a vacation. It was the best vacation ever! One day we got to go on a sailboat. I wanted to go parasailing, but I'm too young... Mom says maybe when I'm older... Everyday we went to the beach. One day we went snorkeling too.

The personal touch

Handwritten **journal** entries emphasize that this is *your* story. Handwriting adds another personal touch to your pages. If you really don't like your handwriting, try this approach.

Write out your thoughts on paper or on the computer. Don't worry about how it looks. The idea at this point is to express yourself. This is a draft, so you can put it away for a while. Take it out later, read it again, and make any changes you want.

Now use good paper and a nice pen to copy the words you wrote. You already decided what to say. Now you can focus on making your handwriting look nice.

Write your journal entry on a computer. Then copy it onto good paper.

Making a Journaling Block

Croppers call the part of the page where you journal a journaling block. To make sure what you write will fit, do your writing first. Then make sure that what you wrote will fit in the space you've allowed. If it won't, you will have to change your layout or write less. Once you know your words will fit, copy the words onto good paper and trim the paper to size.

You can mount the journaling block directly on the page or **mat** it first. To mat it, use the same technique you use to mat photographs.

Apply double-stick tape to the back of the journal entry.

Press the journal entry onto the mat.

Computers & Scrapbooking

Computers are great tools for scrapbooking. Don't go overboard using a computer, though. You don't want your scrapbook pages to lose that personal, handmade feel.

Clip Art

Illustrations that are not protected by copyright are called clip art. They can be used by anyone. Most word processing programs and photo-editing programs come with clip art. After printing an image, you can cut it out and add it to your scrapbook page.

1 In Microsoft® Word software, open a new document. Click "insert" and then "picture" and then "clip art" to access the images.

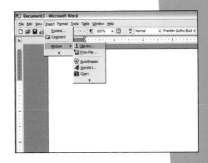

2 To change the size of the illustration once it's in your document, position the cursor over a corner box. Move the box in to make the image smaller. Move it out to make it bigger.

Creating Titles

One easy way to print a title is to type it in a Word document. Highlight the title. Use the menus at the top of the screen to change the font, size, and color.

To change the shape of the letters, use the WordArt function in Word.

Click "View" at the top of the screen. Then click "Toolbars" and then "WordArt." This will open the WordArt toolbar seen here. Click the "insert WordArt" icon.

Select the effect you want. A window will open in which you can type your title and change the font and size. Then you can use the toolbar to change the shape, color, size, and direction of the title.

Journaling

Many people like to do their **journaling** on a computer. To give computer journaling a personal feel, use a font that looks like hand printing.

Drop caps

To **embellish** your journaling, use a **drop cap**.

1 In Word, click "Format" at the top of the screen. Then click "Drop Cap."

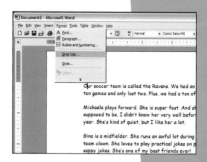

2 Choose the style of drop cap you like from the menu that appears. If you like, choose a decorative font that will be applied to just the drop cap.

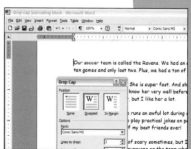

Highlighted Words

Another fun embellishment is to use a different font for some words. Try this with some of the adjectives in your journaling. Highlight the first word you want to stand out. Then use the menus at the top of the screen to change its font and color. Continue highlighting words and changing fonts one word at a time.

Embellishments

Croppers call the decorative touches they add to pages **embellishments**. These include borders, **eyelets**, stickers, **die cuts**, and fibers.

Two-color Border

1 Choose two colors of paper for your border. Cut them to the height you want. The one shown here is one and a half inches (4 cm) high.

2 Use a punch to punch holes in the top layer of paper only. Save the pieces you punch out. Use them somewhere else on the page to continue the theme.

3 Use photo tape to attach the top layer to the under layer. Use more photo tape to attach the completed border to the page.

Eyelets

Eyelets look best when they appear to be holding a photo, title, or other element in place. You can lace yarn or ribbon through eyelets, if you like. Here's how to apply them.

1 Place your page on a hard pounding mat. Make a hole for the eyelet. Position the punch where you want to put the eyelet and tap it with a hammer.

2 Turn the page over. Place the eyelet in the hole from below. Place the end of the setting tool in the back of the eyelet. Tap the setting tool with a hammer until the end of the eyelet flares.

Torn Paper

Using torn paper is a way to emphasize the handmade feel of a page. You can use this technique for **mats**, **journaling** blocks, and paper **embellishments**.

OH, THE PLACES I WILL GO!

1

Mark the tear lines on the paper with a pencil. Use a cotton swab dipped in water to trace over all the lines you made.

2

Hold the "keeper" portion of the paper in your left hand. With your right hand, gently tear along the wet lines. Tear away from yourself if you don't want white edges to show.

3

Tear toward yourself if you do want a white edge to show. If the lines dry out before you finish tearing, dab them again with the cotton swab.

Dry Embossing

An embossed image is one that is raised. You can emboss an image on a small piece of contrasting paper. Then cut it out and attach it to the scrapbook page.

1 Lay the **template** on the light box. If you don't have a light box, use a glass-topped table with a lamp underneath. Place the paper over the template with the top side of the paper facing down.

2 Use the embossing tool to gently rub all over the paper within the outlines of the template. Don't rush, or you may tear the paper. Just keep gently rubbing all over with the embossing tool.

3 Use small scissors to trim the image to size. Leave at least one-eighth inch (3 mm) of flat paper all around the embossed lines. Attach the embossed image to the page with photo tape or spacer tape.

Pocket Pages

Mementos are things that help you remember someone or something. Some examples are ticket stubs, postcards, programs, maps, and brochures.

Mementos like these are a great addition to a scrapbook. But it's also nice to be able to remove them and look at both sides. The ideal solution to this **dilemma** is a pocket page. Here's how to make one.

1

Cut a piece of paper as wide as the page and about five inches (13 cm) high. Apply photo tape to the back along the bottom and side edges. Position the pocket and press firmly along the edges.

2

If you like, punch holes along the sides and bottom of the pocket. Lace yarn or ribbon through the holes. Glue or tape the loose ends to the back of the page.

Glossary

die cut - a decoration made by cutting paper with dies. Dies are steel cutters made to cut paper into a particular shape. Antique die cuts, called scrap, were made in sheets.

dilemma - a problem that requires you to make a difficult choice.

drop cap - a large, decorative letter at the beginning of a paragraph. It is usually as tall as three lines of type. Cap is short for capital.

embellish - to decorate. To make beautiful by adding decorations.

eyelet - a small metal grommet, or ring, used to reinforce a small hole.

journal - a personal record of thoughts, ideas, and experiences. A diary.

mat - a border placed between a picture and its frame. Also, a thick pad used to protect another surface from damage.

pigment - a substance that gives color to other materials. It is often a powder that is added to liquid.

scrap - antique die cuts, advertisements, labels, and cards. The term *scrapbook* comes from the popular Victorian hobby of pasting scrap into blank books.

spread - two facing pages in a book, magazine, or newspaper.

template - a pattern for making something.

vellum - a heavy paper resembling parchment. Vellum was originally made from fine calfskin or lambskin.

Web Sites

To learn more about making scrapbooks, visit ABDO Publishing Company on the World Wide Web at **www.abdopub.com**. Web sites about scrapbooks are featured on our Book Links page. These links are routinely monitored and updated to provide the most current information available.

Index